Smelly Science

Body Odours

COLLEGE OF RIPON
AND YORK ST JOHN
LIBRARY

Dr Peter Rowan

Illustrated by Vince Reid

169270

College of Ripon & York St. John

3 8025 00400713 7

To Dr Bill Hughes

Oxford University Press, Great Clarendon Street, Oxford OX2 6DP

Oxford New York
Athens Auckland Bangkok Bogotá Buenos Aires Calcutta
Cape Town Chennai Dar es Salaam Delhi Florence Hong Kong Istanbul
Karachi Kuala Lumpur Madrid Melbourne Mexico City Mumbai
Nairobi Paris São Paulo Singapore Taipei Tokyo Toronto Warsaw
and associated companies in Berlin Ibadan

Oxford is a registered trade mark of Oxford University Press

Published in the United States
by Oxford University Press Inc., New York

©Dr Peter Rowan 1998
The moral rights of the author have been asserted
First published 1998
The creator of the 'Smelly Science' series concept is Mary Dobson.

Cover artwork by Vince Reid.
Photographs reproduced by kind permission of; p5 Secchi-Lecaque/Roussel-
Uclq-CNRI/SPL; p21 Richard Wehr/SPL; p10 and p18
Prof. P. Motta/University 'La Sapienza" Rome/ SPL.
SPL = Science Photo Library

All rights reserved. No part of this publication may be reproduced,
stored in a retrieval system, or transmitted, in any form or by any means,
without the prior permission in writing of Oxford University Press.
Within the UK, exceptions are allowed in respect of any fair dealing for the
purpose of research or private study, or criticism or review, as permitted
under the Copyright, Designs and Patents Act 1988, or in the case of
reprographic reproduction in accordance with the terms of the licences
issued by the Copyright Licensing Agency. Enquiries concerning
reproduction outside these terms and in other countries should be
sent to the Rights Department, Oxford University Press,
at the address above

This book is sold subject to the condition that it shall not, by way
of trade or otherwise, be lent, re-sold, hired out or otherwise circulated
without the publisher's prior consent in any form of binding or cover
other than that in which it is published and without a similar condition
including this condition being imposed on the subsequent purchaser

British Library Cataloguing
in Publication Data available

ISBN 0 19 9105731

1 3 5 7 9 10 8 6 4 2

Printed in Great Britain

Contents

Science Makes Sense 4

Brilliant Brains 6

Senses Make Sense 8

Easy Breathing 12

Stopping the Rot 14

Disgusting Digestion 16

Getting to the Bottom 18

Sweaty Skin 20

Mighty Movers 22

Pungent Pee 24

Deadly Defences 26

Dreadful Diseases 28

Pungent Puzzles 30

Glossary 31

Index 32

Scratch and sniff the scented panels lightly with a fingernail
to release their smell.

Science Makes Sense

Oily armpits, sweaty skin, cheesy feet and bad breath — no matter how much you drench yourself in deodorant or gargle with minty mouthwash, you can't escape it: your body smells! But these odours and pongs are not just skin deep. They are part of the processes that make your body such an amazing machine that performs thousands of different tasks, every second of every day of your life.

Science explains the world around you — both what you can see and what is hidden, the living, and the non-living. It's a wonderful mix of facts and figures, experiments and observations - science can be fun! And, as you're about to find out, it can also be smelly!

Your incredible body is made of thousands of parts, from the tiniest bone in your ear to your 8-metre long intestine. This book will whizz you round to see how it really works. But beware, there's some pretty whiffy stuff ahead. To make sense of your body, you've got to use your sense of smell!

Body building

All the organs in your body, like your heart, lungs and brain, are made from tissues, which in turn are built from cells, the basic building blocks of all bodies. Your body's 50,000 billion cells, are constantly dying and being replaced. Different cells do different jobs, but whether it's a skin cell on your freshly scrubbed face or a smell cell inside your nose, their basic design is the same.

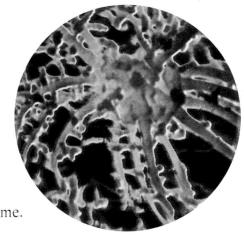

A smell cell! This is where the whole smelly story begins - up your nose!

Your breathtaking body

Your body is really just a collection of chemicals: carbon, oxygen, hydrogen, nitrogen, sulphur and phosphorus. A newborn baby is 75% water! Yet your body achieves amazing things. During your lifetime you will eat for nearly three and a half years, produce 40,000 litres of urine and spend over six months on the loo. You produce 200 billion red blood cells every day, and can tell the difference between millions of different colours. What a breathtaking body!

From your body you could make a small iron nail, 9,000 pencil leads, seven bars of soap, a jar of sugar, enough sulphur to kill all the fleas on a dog, 2,000 phosphorus match heads, three buckets of water and enough hydrogen to fill a balloon that could lift you to the top of the Eiffel Tower!

5

Brilliant Brains

What looks like a watery, wrinkled, pink-grey blancmange, is small enough to hold in your hand, yet is probably the most powerful and complex tissue on Earth? Your brain! It's the headquarters of your body, that makes everything happen. Because of it you can smell that rotting banana at the bottom of your school bag, name all the players in your favourite football team, ride your bike – even understand this book!

Sensuous pleasures
Sight, hearing, touch, taste and smell — all your senses report back to the brain. But your sense of smell is surely the most powerful. Babies rely on smell as soon as they are born, to find their mother's milk. Unlike the other senses, smell is plugged directly into the emotional part of your brain. A mother very soon knows her new baby by its smell — it encourages them to cuddle and bond together.

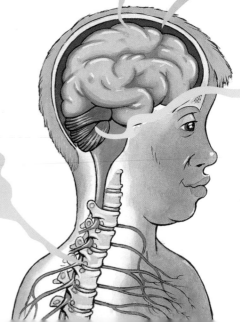

Your brilliant brain is linked through your spinal cord by nerves to just about every other part of your body. Messages whizz in and out of it at 360 km per hour - phew!

Thinking
All your thoughts, however daft, come from your brain. If you feel 'a bundle of nerves' just before a race, or amazingly happy when you get what you want for your birthday, that's your brain at work.

Magical memory
I'm sure you know how to tie your shoelaces. And you probably know how to ride a bike. These skills are difficult to forget. They are stored in your long-term memory. But fact memories, like history dates and telephone numbers, slip away much more easily. They may only stay in your short-term memory. Smell can bring back memories from the past. Does one sniff of freshly mown grass remind you of summer?

Movement
It's your brain that sends messages to your muscles so that they move the way you want. Every twitch of your nose, every blink of your eye — in fact every move you make — is controlled by your brain.

Balance
Two small brain computers at the back of your head control your balance, to stop you falling over. So you should be able to avoid a disgusting dip!

Breathtaking Body Facts

- You have more than 100,000,000,000 nerve cells inside your head.

- Your brain's power is awesome, but incredibly it runs on just 80 grams of sugar a day, and uses less energy than a bedroom night light!

- For such an amazing organ, your brain is remarkably thick-skinned. In fact, it can't feel a thing. You could cut it in half and it would feel no pain.

Senses Make Sense

Delicious doughnuts, fluffy fur, colourful cartoons, twittering bluetits and sizzling sausages — you gather all the sensations from the wonderful world around you using your five senses. Without sight, hearing, touch, taste or smell, you would be completely cut off. So don't be in the dark — make sense of your senses with this story.

Daisy can smell something cooking. **SCRATCH AND SNIFF for a yummy whiff and get those tastebuds twitching.** Daisy creeps from her cosy warm bed onto the cold floor. It's dark, but she has the light of the moon to help her see.

Light rays from an object enter your eyes through the pupils. They form a picture at the back of the eye, which sends messages to your brain, so that you can see the object.

You feel through millions of tiny sensors in your skin, called nerve endings. These can tell the difference between hot and cold, hard and soft. They also tell you about pain!

Daisy feels her way in the dark, – and steps on her hairbrush – ouch! What's that? Just an owl hooting.

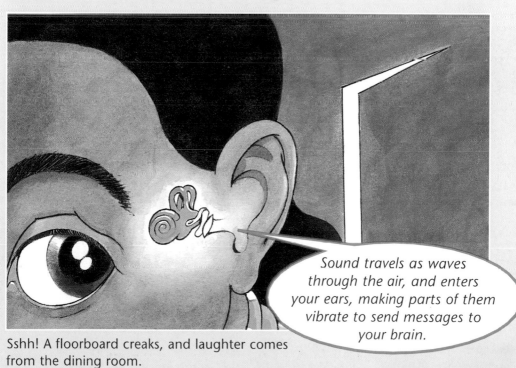

Sound travels as waves through the air, and enters your ears, making parts of them vibrate to send messages to your brain.

Sshh! A floorboard creaks, and laughter comes from the dining room.

Daisy follows her nose to the yummy food.
She takes a good sniff - mmm!

When you breathe in, smells get sucked into your nose, where they meet smell 'sensors'. These send messages to your brain, which tells you what you've sniffed.

You taste with taste buds on your tongue. Your tongue can detect four kinds of taste: bitter, sweet, sour and salty. Taste and smell are closely linked. When you have a cold and your nose is blocked, it's very hard to taste your food - you might as well be eating cotton wool!

This is what your tongue looks like up-close!

Smelly signals

Where would we be without smell? This powerful sense helps us with some pretty basic activities and feelings. How can you tell the toast is burning, while you're deep in reading this book? How can you tell the meat's rotten and poisonous? How are we attracted to each other? Smell is a 'distance' sense, which gives us early warnings of dangers or attractions — definitely a talent not to be sniffed at!

Nasty noses

The Mayor of Angoulême, during the French Revolution, had a nose weighing almost 1 kg. To breathe he had to lean forwards, and when he ate, someone else had to hold it for him. At night, he kept it in a sling tied to his nightcap!

The longest human nose ever known belonged to an Englishman called Thomas Wedders (left). It was almost 20cm long!

Our noses are in just the right place on our face — you can keep an eye on food going in, and poke your nose in wherever you fancy before the rest of your face arrives.

Most of us can distinguish 4,000 different smells. Trained 'noses' can tell up to 10,000 — very useful for the makers of perfumes, soaps and wines.

Talented tongues

A baby has over 10,000 taste buds on its tongue; an old person has about 5,000.

Easy Breathing

What happens when you smell? Your friends run away from you, of course! No, when you smell something? When you sniff the fragrant perfume of a lovely garden, or the pungent pong of a pigsty, you are really breathing in. All day and all night, your two lungs pump air in and out of your chest, to get the gas oxygen into your body, and another gas, carbon dioxide, out of it. This work is done by a large flat muscle in your chest, called the diaphragm, which moves up and down, drawing the air in or pushing it out.

When you take a breath through your nose or mouth and fill your lungs with air, oxygen passes into your blood. Why do you need oxygen? You use it to unlock the energy from the food you eat. In the process, carbon dioxide is produced, which you breathe out.

Scratch and sniff for an airy whiff. Can't smell anything? That's because oxygen has no smell!

Your leaky lungs are wired by nerves to your brilliant brain, to control the rate of breathing. If there's too much carbon dioxide in the blood, your brain makes you breathe faster to get rid of it. This is all done automatically, so you don't have to worry about breathing faster while running a race. Or even remembering to breathe while asleep!

Inside your lungs are about 300 million tiny air sacs, called alveoli. Oxygen and carbon dioxide pass between the air in your lungs and the blood, through tiny blood vessels called capillaries.

Running away from the world's worst smell needs big breaths.

Top Tip for a Long Healthy Life

Don't stop breathing.

Breathtaking Body Facts

- Air can move in and out of the lungs at different speeds. Clock these on the Sniff-O-Metre:

- In a normal day you breathe in up to 20,000 litres of air.

- Even if you spent all day in bed you'd still breathe 8,000 litres of air to stay alive.

- Sticky mucus moistens and warms the air up your nose. Every day you make a disgusting litre of hot snot!

- The epiglottis is a trap door to stop food going into your lungs instead of your stomach. Anything that goes the wrong way gets blasted out by a cough.

- If you ironed all your alveoli out flat they would cover at least half a tennis court.

- If you could throw your air-filled lungs into the bath they would float. (Don't try this one at home.) They are the only part of the human body that's light enough to do this!

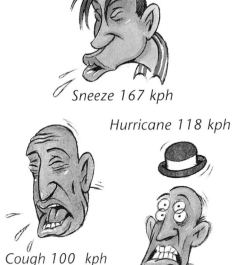

Sneeze 167 kph

Hurricane 118 kph

Cough 100 kph

Hiccup 80 kph

Sniff 70 kph

Laugh (good one) 25 kph

Talking 18 kph

Yawn 15 kph

Breathing (asleep) 8 kph

Snore 10 kph

13

Stopping the Rot

You need fresh flesh to stay alive. Blood and oxygen keep you smelling fragrant. If any part of the body gets cut off from its blood supply, the tissue starts to die. This revolting rot is called gangrene – and it stinks. The heart may be linked to love, but there's certainly no amorous aroma when flesh starts to fester.

While you've been reading, your body's been busy. By the time you've read the paragraph above, some of your 30,000 billion red blood cells have travelled right round your body, pumped from the heart. The blood flowed through tubes called blood vessels. The whole process took about one minute.

Billy blood cell has just filled up with oxygen at Lung Airport. Oxygen has just flown in with the last breath. Billy's passed through Harry Heart, and is now being pumped down an artery, one of the three types of blood vessels that go round the body.

First stop on Billy's circulatory route of tissues and organs is Kathy Kidney. Here Billy unloads the oxygen ordered by Kathy, and picks up the unwanted carbon dioxide, which he will take back to the heart.

Billy's on his way back to Harry Heart through the veins. He'll then push on back to Lung Airport to deliver his load of carbon dioxide, where it will be on the next breath out of town.

Smelly Old Iron

Your body needs iron. It uses it to make haemoglobin, the stuff in blood cells that carries the oxygen. This is what makes blood red! Iron is a mineral, and you need a balanced diet to get enough of it. Peanuts, chocolate and baked beans on brown toast have lots of it – sounds OK! So do green vegetables, boiled eggs and sardines – yuk!

Breathtaking Body Facts

- Laid end to end, the blood vessels in your body would go round the world at least twice.
- More than 2 million blood cells are destroyed and replaced every second.
- Your heart is a muscle that never stops moving while you are alive.

Disgusting Digestion

hat did you have for breakfast today? Whatever it was, it's now gurgling its way through your system. When your nostrils start twitching, and your tummy starts rumbling, the great, gruesome, digestion train is about to depart... It's pretty revolting, so take a deep breath before we start, and definitely don't try eating while you're reading...

The succulent smell of breakfast sets saliva swirling around your mouth.

Food is chomped and chewed by teeth, and mixed with saliva to begin its digestion.

The swallowed breakfast is now in your stomach, being churned around with gastric juices. Stomach acid is so strong it could burn a hole in a carpet. Luckily your stomach wall has a sticky mucous coating to protect it! If something harmful goes in - it'll try to get out again! You start to sweat, you make more saliva (to protect your teeth from the acid in vomit), you breathe more quickly, your chest muscles contract and - uurgh! - it's out!

Muscles in the gut wall have squeezed breakfast, which is now like a mushy soup, down to the small intestine. This is a coiled tube about 6 metres long, where most of the goodies in the food are absorbed into your body. But now your stomach's feeling empty again. Time for more grub!

Burping brings up air from the stomach. Depending on what's inside, this may not smell so sweet! You may think that garlic tasted good in a burger last night, but when it comes back up as a burp next day not everyone will agree with you.

Scratch and sniff for a stale garlicky whiff.

Foul foods

In some parts of the world, these are considered delicious: raw ducks' feet, caterpillars, flying ants and fruit bats.

Lovely liver

Your liver is a large chemical factory in your body. It breaks down your food, and destroys poisons like alcohol.

Getting to the Bottom

Your large intestine is without doubt the smelliest part of your body. It is a coiled tube nearly 2 metres long, that carries what's left of digested food from the small intestine to the hole in your bottom (anus). As this waste moves towards the exit, much of the water in it is absorbed back into your body. This makes it more solid. Normally the whiffy waste arrives at the end of its journey about 18 hours after the original meal, and you feel the need to get rid of it — hopefully in a convenient place nearby.

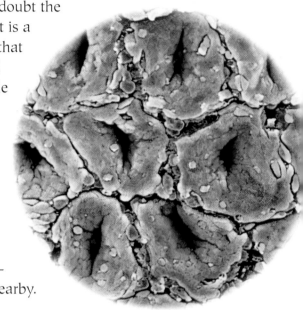

Inside your large intestine, these cells absorb the water from your waste!

Goodbye! The remains of yesterday's lunch finally make their exit.

About 12 times a day your body needs to 'let off' some of the stinky gas in the large intestine. This is usually called farting. Some of it is air you swallowed with the food, the rest is gas formed as the food was broken down by tiny bacteria in the intestine. You probably release about 500 ml of gas every day — enough to fill a milk bottle.

'Baked-beans-on-toast day.'

'Meat-and-two-vegetables day.'

So what's in a fart? A typical one contains 60% nitrogen, 20% hydrogen, and 20% carbon dioxide, methane, oxygen, and hydrogen sulphide. But the contents vary depending on what you've eaten. Eating beans produces a gas that is mostly hydrogen — this one's noisy rather than smelly. But scoffing meat has quite a different effect. Meat contains sulphur, which combines with hydrogen in your intestine to make hydrogen sulphide — otherwise known to its few friends as 'rotten eggs' — *phew!*

A painful record

The world record for constipation is held by Emily Plumley, born in 1850. She waited to go for 102 days!

Sweaty Skin

You smell! Not surprising, since the outer layer of the skin bag you live in is dead. When you scratch your nose or shake hands with a teacher, you are feeling dead tissue! This outer skin layer (epidermis) is a collection of millions of cells. They are growing this minute, and working their way up towards the surface, where they fall off into your bed, classroom, carpet and everywhere else. We are surrounded by everybody's dead skin — yuk!

This dead layer stops you getting a dirty dermis — the inner layer of the skin. This has all the blood vessels and nerves. Your skin is huge — 75 million million cells, weighing 4 kg. No wonder it is your body's record holder for the heaviest organ!

Nerve endings in your skin make you feel heat and cold, light or deep touch, and pain. A sloppy kiss is a mixture of touch and heat!

Stay cool!
Your sweaty skin helps control your body's temperature. Run a race and the skin's sweat glands ooze salty water. As this evaporates into the air it makes you feel cooler. This is why you sweat more on a hot day, or after playing games.

Phew ! - scratch and sniff for a sweat-soaked whiff.

Beastly bugs

You share your skin with millions of mouldy microbes. There are 3 million of them just on your face! There are enough hiding in every nook and cranny of your skin to fill a teacup. And your skin bugs love sweat! Especially the really sweaty bits like feet and armpits. Sweat smells fabulous when it's fresh, but if you don't wash it off the bugs multiply on it, and turn it into a wickedly rotten body odour.

A dust mite feeds on bits of dead skin.

Blood keeps your skin alive. When you're cold it moves away from the skin surface to save heat, so you go paler. When you're warm, you go red as the blood moves towards the skin surface to lose heat. When you're cold your hairs stand on end, to trap the warm air near your skin and so keep in the heat.

Breathtaking Body Facts

- Every body has 2.5 million sweat glands. Each gland is 5 mm long, so you have over 10 km of sweat glands.

- Some of the pint of sweat we make every day seeps out through the soles of our feet. Dogs can track humans from their footprints because of this — even if they're wearing shoes.

- Nails and hair are modified bits of skin. They are all made of the same substance — keratin. It's just harder in some places than others.

- Our smelly scent glands are in our armpits and groins. Other animals have them in peculiar places. The rhino has them in its feet, the elephant in its forehead, and the rabbit in its bottom!

Mighty Movers

Sometimes we need to move — fast! Whether it's away from a stinking drain or towards that last delicious cake, we need our bones and muscles to allow us to get about. Your skeleton is the scaffolding on which all your other body parts hang. And your muscles move the bones at their joints.

Muscles are responsible for every move you make, both those you do on purpose, like reaching, twisting and leaping, and those you do without thinking, like breathing! Moving those muscles can make some pretty potent pongs!

Muscles shorten when they move you. They can only pull, they can't push, so another muscle must pull the other way to make the opposite movement. These muscles are moving your funny bone, but if you hit it, you definitely won't be laughing....

Breathtaking Body Facts

- It takes 47 muscles to frown, but only 17 to smile, so save energy – be happy!

- There are over 600 muscles and 200 bones in your body, so you can move just about any which way you choose.

- Did you know you have muscles in your ears? Try wiggling them. Most people have forgotten how to use them. If you stop using a muscle it shrinks and becomes useless, just like the wing muscles of penguins — they never fly.

Revolting reflexes

Sniff a pile of rotting cabbage. Step on a pin. Touch a hot iron. Your muscles will move you away from harm's way in the blink of an eye. These are the body's protective reflexes, working even before your brain realizes you are in danger.

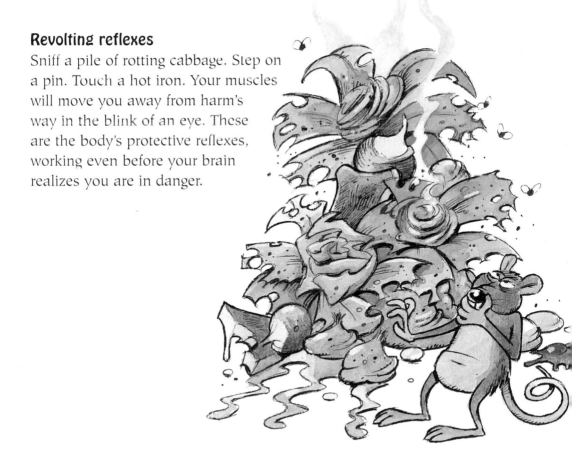

Pungent Pee

Ancient people used it as soap. In South America it has been used as a mouthwash and a refreshing drink. Every day you pass about 1.5 litres of the stuff. Yes, it's urine — that strange pale yellow liquid that is continually being filtered from your blood by your two kidneys. What is it exactly? How do we make it? And does it really smell so bad?

Urine is really just water with waste material from the body dissolved in it. Every day we take in 2 to 3 litres of fluids, as drinks and in food. This is quickly absorbed by your body into your blood.

Blood is being filtered by your two kidneys all the time. Every minute of every day, one fifth of all the blood in your body is being filtered by your kidneys. A kidney is a mass of over a million tiny tubes, that filter out some of the water in your blood and make urine out of it. Most of the water is returned to the body. (If this didn't happen, you'd be peeing all day, and drinking constantly to replace the water!) The urine passes to the bladder. This muscular sac slowly fills up like a balloon.

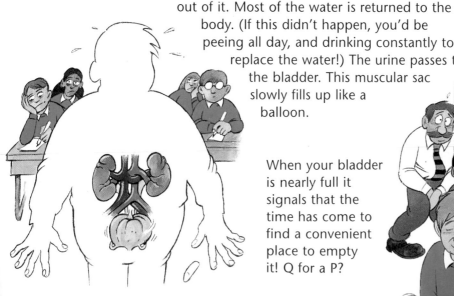

When your bladder is nearly full it signals that the time has come to find a convenient place to empty it! Q for a P?

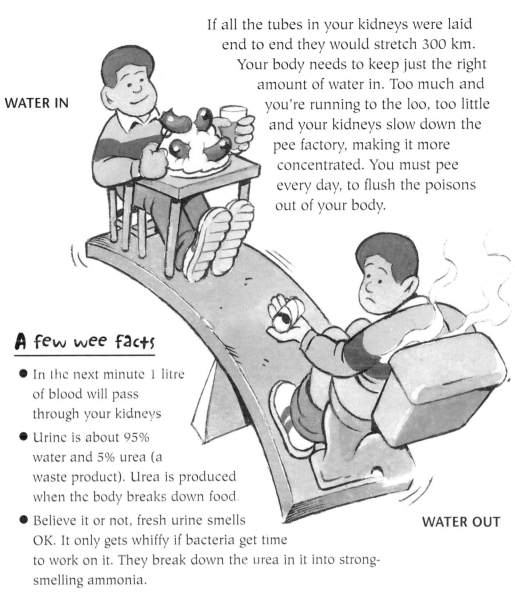

WATER IN

If all the tubes in your kidneys were laid end to end they would stretch 300 km. Your body needs to keep just the right amount of water in. Too much and you're running to the loo, too little and your kidneys slow down the pee factory, making it more concentrated. You must pee every day, to flush the poisons out of your body.

A few wee facts

- In the next minute 1 litre of blood will pass through your kidneys

- Urine is about 95% water and 5% urea (a waste product). Urea is produced when the body breaks down food.

- Believe it or not, fresh urine smells OK. It only gets whiffy if bacteria get time to work on it. They break down the urea in it into strong-smelling ammonia.

WATER OUT

- An average adult body contains about 40 litres of water — that's enough for you to have a bath in — IF you wanted.

- By the age of 70 you will have passed over 38,000 litres of urine — enough to flood a football pitch!

- You can live for a month without food, but only a few days without water.

Deadly Defences

Have you ever had a putrid cut? The kind that gets all hot and oozes disgusting yellow pus? If you have, you've seen your body's defences in action. Pus is a mixture of the evil invader germs and your white blood cells which rush up to attack them.

Terrible Tetanus and his friends Dirt and Muck live in this stinky ditch. Along comes a nice clean foot and cuts itself on some rusty metal. Tetanus and Dirt can't wait to dash into the wound.

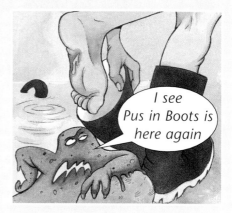

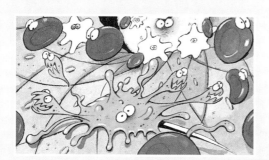

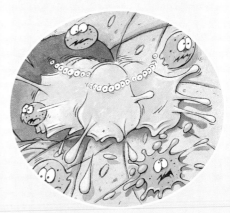

In seconds, the ghastly germs enter through the skin. The outer wall of the body's defences have been breached! Terrible Tetanus and his mucky mates start to multiply. Alarm bells ring at the nearest guard post - one of the lymph nodes positioned around the body.

The protection police are on the prowl, frantically making rockets of bug busters to fire at the germs. Luckily for the body, he was sent secret plans to protect him against this invasion years ago (vaccination at school), so he has the right weapon for Terrible Tetanus.

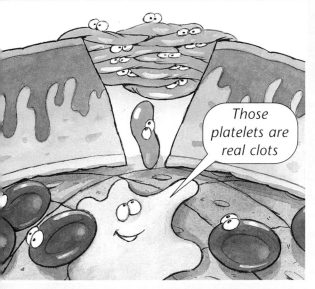

Those platelets are real clots

We're cell mates from now on

Meanwhile, small particles called platelets plug the gap and help to make the blood set, stopping the wound from bleeding.

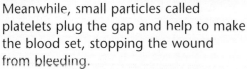

Soldiers arrive in tanks to round up a few stragglers who have escaped into the surrounding tissue. The invasion is over, the battle is won. The monstrous microbes are either dead or in prison. The skin wall is under repair, with temporary scab cover.

Back in the spleen, damaged and old cells are removed from the blood. New white blood cells are being made to fight on another day.

Dreadful Diseases

Some of the nastiest diseases smell the worst! This is handy, as it helps us avoid them. But the poor citizens of the city of Kaffa in Crimea couldn't get out of the way when their city was under siege in the 14th century. The Tartar attackers couldn't break down the city's walls, so they catapulted the rotting corpses of plague victims over the top, into the streets. The citizens of Kaffa caught the disease and died — a mouldy early example of germ warfare.

Our normally sweat-smelling bodies can become very smelly indeed when things go wrong with them. Even in these high-tech. days, doctors still follow their noses. . .

Dr N. Parker will now try to sniff out some disgusting diseases. Each has its own particular smell.

Yellow fever (a bloody butcher's shop)

Smallpox (sweaty geese)

Typhoid fever (newly baked bread)

German measles (a freshly plucked chicken)

No flies on him

Even insects are into smells! Fruit flies like the smell of patients with liver disease, and will gather around their beds!

Rotten remedies

In the past, people thought foul smells gave some protection against the plague. Englishmen slept with unwashed goats, or kept their heads down the privy during the day. Phew!

Here are some more terrible traditional remedies:

Cramp
Carry a mole's foot

Bad breath and headaches
Blow tobacco smoke up the bottom

Boils
Put a live chicken (without
tail feathers) on them

Whooping cough
Drink owl soup

Dog bite
Apply a hair of the dog quickly

Mumps
Walk three times aound a pigsty

Epilepsy
Drink fresh gladiator blood

Pungent Puzzles

1. Why is blood red?
a) because oxygen is red
b) because of a pigment in red blood cells
c) so you know when you've cut yourself

2. Which of these gases makes farts smell?
a) carbon di-backside
b) methane
c) sulphur bog-oxide

3. What is the capital of France?
a) Sydney (Gladys if he's away)
b) Paris
c) Smelly sock

Awful anagrams

Rearrange these letters to make:

A long coiled tube that takes your food from one end to the other — **NITSINEET**

Stinking rotting body tissue — **ANEGRENG**

A pongy liquid that gives this book its name — **WESTA**

Answers:
1. b) Haemoglobin is red
2. b)
3 b) A trick question. If you find the answer funny, then my brain and yours have shared a uniquely human experience – humour. As far as we know, no other animal possesses this way of thinking.

Glossary

alveoli tiny air sacs in the lungs

blood red liquid that flows round the body in blood vessels. Red blood cells carry oxygen, white blood cells fight infection, and platelets help stop cuts bleeding.

blood vessels the tubes that carry blood around the body. Arteries carry blood away from the heart, veins carry it back to the heart, and capillaries are tiny tubes linking arteries and veins.

carbon dioxide a waste gas produced by the body

cell a microscopic building block of the body

constipation a delay in emptying the bowels

dermis the inner layer of the skin

diaphragm a flat muscle under the lungs, used when we breathe

epidermis the outer layer of the skin

epiglottis a firm flap of tissue behind the tongue, to keep food out of the lungs

gangrene when part of the body dies because of poor blood supply

haemoglobin a substance with iron, found in red blood cells

intestines a digestive tube about 8 metres long which goes from the stomach to the anus

keratin a hard substance found in nails, hair and the outer layer of the skin

lymph node a small collection of body defence cells

microbes small germs

nerves fibres that carry messages round the body to and from the brain

organ a body part, eg brain, liver, heart or kidney

oxygen a gas in the air which we need to breathe to live

reflexes fast and automatic reactions of the body, eg blinking

saliva a fluid created by glands around the face and passed into the mouth to start the breakdown of food

sensation an experience produced by one of the senses: smell, sight, touch, hearing and taste

tetanus a serious infection of the nerves, causing violent muscle spasm

urine the watery liquid made by the kidneys from blood and stored in the bladder

Index

babies 5, 6

bacteria 19, 21, 26, 27

balance 7

blood 5, 12, 14-15, 20, 21, 24,
      25, 27

bones 4, 22, 23

brain 5, 6-7, 8, 9, 10, 12, 23

breathing 4, 10, 12-13

carbon 5

carbon dioxide 12, 14, 19

cells 5, 7, 14, 20

digestion 16-17, 18-19

disease 26-27, 28-29

excretion 18, 19

feet 4

hearing 6, 8, 9

heart 5, 14-15

hydrogen 5, 19

infection 26-27

intestines 4, 17, 18, 19

iron 5, 15

kidneys 14, 24, 25

liver 17, 29

lungs 5, 12, 13, 14

memory 7

movement 7, 22-23

muscles 7, 15, 17, 22-23

nerves 6, 7, 9, 12, 20

nitrogen 5, 19

oxygen 5, 12, 14, 19

phosphorus 5

reflexes 23

senses 6, 8-9, 10-11

sight 6, 8

skin 4, 5, 20-21

smell 4, 5, 6, 7, 8, 10, 11, 12-13,
      16, 19, 20, 21, 23, 28-29

spleen 27

stomach 16, 17

sulphur 5

sweat 4, 20-21

taste 6, 8, 10

teeth 16

tongue 10, 11

touch 6, 8, 23

urine 24-25